**W9-DAX-695**

# Going by Bus

by Susan Ashley

Reading consultant: Susan Nations, M.Ed., author/literacy coach/consultant

Please visit our web site at: **www.earlyliteracy.cc**
For a free color catalog describing Weekly Reader® Early Learning Library's
list of high-quality books, call 1-877-445-5824 (USA) or 1-800-387-3178 (Canada).
Weekly Reader® Early Learning Library's fax: (414) 336-0164.

**Library of Congress Cataloging-in-Publication Data**

Ashley, Susan.
    Going by bus / by Susan Ashley.
      p. cm. — (Going places)
    Includes bibliographical references and index.
    ISBN 0-8368-3729-0 (lib. bdg.)
    ISBN 0-8368-3834-3 (softcover)
    1. Buses—Juvenile literature. 2. Bus travel—Juvenile literature. [1. Buses.
  2. Bus travel.] I. Title.
  TL232.A84   2003
  629.222'33—dc21
                                    2003045024

This edition first published in 2004 by
**Weekly Reader® Early Learning Library**
330 West Olive Street, Suite 100
Milwaukee, WI 53212 USA

Art direction: Tammy Gruenewald
Photo research: Diane Laska-Swanke
Editorial assistant: Erin Widenski
Cover and layout design: Katherine A. Goedheer

Photo credits: Cover, title, p. 17 © Gibson Stock Photography; pp. 4, 6, 7, 8, 9, 10,
12, 13, 14, 15, 16, 19 (left), 20, 21 © Gregg Andersen; pp. 5, 18 © Kim Karpeles;
p. 11 Manhattan Bus Map © Metropolitan Transportation Authority. Used with permission.;
p. 19 (right) © North Wind Picture Archives

Printed in the United States of America

1 2 3 4 5 6 7 8 9 07 06 05 04 03

# Table of Contents

School buses bring children to school every day.

## School Buses

How did you get to school today?  Did you
ride a bus to school?  Millions of children
ride buses to school each day.  School
buses take children to school in the city,
in the suburbs, and in the country.

All school buses are painted a special shade of yellow. When other drivers see this color, they know it is a school bus and they must drive carefully. Yellow is a safe color because it is easy to see, even on a rainy or snowy day. Can you think of other vehicles that are painted bright colors?

**All school buses are painted yellow.**

The driver of this school bus has stopped traffic so children crossing the street will be safe.

A school bus has other safety features. When a school bus stops to pick you up or drop you off, red lights flash on the front and back of the bus. A red "STOP" sign swings out from the left side of the bus.

Other cars must stop when they see the flashing lights and stop sign. They cannot pass the bus or drive around it. The flashing lights and stop sign help you stay safe as you get on or off the bus.

**The stop sign and flashing red lights on this school bus mean one thing – STOP!**

**Staying seated and facing forward is the safe way to ride the bus.**

The bus driver's job is to keep you safe. The bus driver is trained to drive safely. Talking loudly or making too much noise will distract the driver.  It is important to stay in your seat and face forward while the bus is moving.

At the end of the school day, the bus will take you home. Hold the handrail and be careful as you leave the bus. Step away from the bus so the driver can see you. If you need to cross the street, wait until the bus driver gives you the signal that it is safe to cross.

**These children are being careful as they get off the school bus.**

This city bus is extra long. It bends in
the middle when it goes around corners.

## City Buses

City buses are busy day and night. A city
bus takes people to work and home again.
People in a city can ride the bus to visit
their friends or go shopping. They can
ride the bus to a museum or a movie.

Each city bus has its own route and schedule. A route map shows where each bus goes. A schedule shows what time the bus arrives at each stop. City bus stops are marked with signs on the curb.

**This is a route map for a city bus in parts of New York City.**

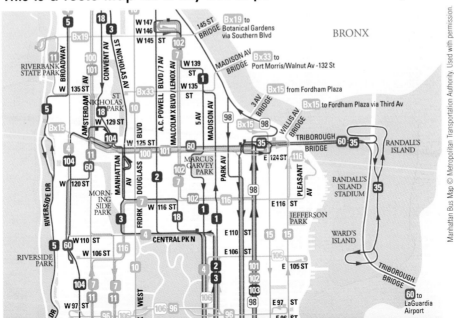

**Most passengers must pay a fare to ride a city bus.**

Passengers pay money, called a **fare**, when they board the bus. When they are ready to get off the bus, they can push a button or pull a cord. This makes a sound and tells the driver that someone is getting off at the next stop.

Some city buses have a "passenger lift" that helps a person in a wheelchair get on and off the bus. Other buses can be lowered in front to make it easier to board the bus. These are called "kneeling" buses.

**This bus has a special lift to help people get on and off the bus.**

Long-distance buses take people all over the country.

## Long-distance Buses

Long-distance buses travel all over America. They travel to large cities and to small towns. Some go all the way across the country. It takes three days for a bus to travel from New York City to Los Angeles.

Long-distance buses pick up passengers at a bus terminal. Passengers can buy their tickets at the terminal before they board the bus. If you look at the front of a bus, you can tell where it is going. A sign above the windshield shows its final destination.

The sign on the front of this bus shows where the bus is going.

**Passengers sit up high on the top level of this motorcoach.**

A bus designed for long-distance travel is called a **motorcoach**. A motorcoach is taller than a city bus or a school bus. It has two levels. Passengers sit on the top level. Luggage is stored on the bottom level.

Some long-distance bus companies offer tours of scenic or historic parts of the country. Some operate charter buses. Charter buses are motorcoaches hired to take a group of people to a special event.

**A charter bus can be hired for special trips.**

It is fun to sit on the top level of a double-decker bus!

## Special Buses

There are many other types of buses. People who want to tour a city and see its sights can take a sightseeing bus. Some sightseeing buses have seating on two levels. These are called double-decker buses.

Some cities use trolley buses for sightseeing. A trolley bus looks like an old-fashioned streetcar. Streetcars were the original city buses. They moved on tracks and sometimes were pulled by horses.

**Riding a modern trolley bus (left) feels a lot like riding an old-fashioned streetcar (right).**

This shuttle bus takes people back and forth between the airport and the parking lot.

Shuttle buses carry people back and forth between two points or along a fixed route. Shuttle buses are busy at airports, where they carry people between the airport and a parking lot or hotel.

Some of the National Parks have shuttle buses. Visitors use the buses to travel through the parks. With fewer cars on the roads, there is less traffic and less air pollution. This is an example of how buses help both people and the environment!

**Public parks use shuttle buses to move people from one place to another.**

# Glossary

**distract** — to draw people's attention away from what they are doing

**environment** — natural surroundings, including air, land, and water

**fare** — the price a person pays to travel

**motorcoach** — a large bus with seats on the top level and luggage space on the bottom level

**old-fashioned** — like styles of the past

**route** — a course of travel or regular round of stops

**scenic** — having natural beauty

**sightseeing** — visiting places of interest

**suburbs** — an area of homes close to a city

# For More Information

**Books**

Gorman, Jacqueline Laks. *Bus Driver*. Milwaukee: Weekly Reader Early Learning Library, 2002.

Klingel, Cynthia and Robert B. Noyed. *School Buses*. Chanhassen: The Child's World, 2000.

Raatma, Lucia. *Safety on the School Bus*. Mankato: Bridgestone Books, 1999.

Ready, Dee. *School Buses*. Mankato: Bridgestone Books, 1997.

**Web Sites**

**Greyhound**
www.greyhound.com/
Click on "Travel Planning" and then "Greyhound Experience" for photos, route maps, and other information on long-distance bus travel.

**New York City Buses**
www.nycsubway.org/bus/
Photo gallery of city buses

**School Bus & School Zone Safety Kids Page**
www.nysgtsc.state.ny.us/kid-schl.htm
School bus safety

# Index